The Heart of Winter

ANN FENELON

To order additional copies of this book, contact:
Xlibris
844-714-8691
www.Xlibris.com
Orders@Xlibris.com

ISBN: Softcover   978-1-6641-9565-3
           Hardcover   978-1-6641-9566-0
           EBook   978-1-6641-9567-7

Library of Congress Control Number: 2021921546

Print information available on the last page

Rev. date: 10/21/2021

DEDICATION

This book is dedicated to my mother,

Isabella D. Fenelon -- still missed and remembered with a love that never dies.

The Heart Of Winter

I sat quietly late last night,
To hear, the sound,
Of snow falling on snow.

One would think it makes no sound.
Snow falling on snow.
But, it speaks in quiet whispers.

Like the voice of God.
One must listen with the heart.
Discern, the inaudible

Through the soul.
Listen to a solitary,
Flake find its mate.

To reunite winter after winter.
To bond, to become whole again.
Lovers who have concurred,

The bounds of time.
To live again, to love again.
Is the sound of snow falling on snow.

A.T.F.
"the poet"

Pink Rose

Pale moon rose
Sweetest flower
That grows.

Fragrant rose
Perfumed blossom.
Heaven's bloom;

To see you is a
Blessing-
To hold you divine.

I adore from afar,
Worship you in my
 Heart,

And hunger for you
In my soul;
In the core of me,

In the very core
Of me-
You are growing.

Ann T. Fenelon
11-07-01

Just Because

Just because I see you
I smile.
Just because I'm near
You- I laugh.
Just because of you.

A raining day has no
Hold on me.
The cold is warmth
To me,
Just because of you.

Night is day to me;
Sun is moon to me.
Stars just shine-
Rainbows rhyme,
Just because of you.

Time has no hold on me.
Space gets lost inside-
The soul of me,
And my heart beats-
Just because of you.

In time I know you'll
See.
Life's no good without
Me.
Just because of you.

11-6-01

Four Roses

The White Rose is the symbol-
Of hope and purity, and innocents;

The Yellow Rose is the symbol-
Of deep and abiding friendship,
More powerful and poignant,
Then a dozen RED;

The Pink Rose is the symbol-
Of heart felt passion,
All consuming, in its fire;

The Red Rose is the symbol-
Of true Love-
Eternal Love-
It is a combination of the three.

The hope of purity and innocents,
Powerful and poignant, friendship,
And consuming passion-
That burns in its desire.

These Roses grow for you-
In the garden of my heart,
Pluck them one by one.

A.T.F.
11-17-01

A Hole In My Heart

There is a hole in my heart;
Where love once lived,
An abyss that time can never heal.

I look for you face in every crowed.
I hear you voice in the whisper of the wind.
When I close my eyes to sleep,

I find you there.
Your beautiful face, smiling at me,
Your soft lips, calling out my name,

For you now exist only in dreams.
And there is a hole in my heart.
An abyss of unspoken sorrow,

A madness that lives as grief,
And a pain that numbs the soul,
Are the gifts of your abandoned.

How can I be whole again.
What will make me whole.
Who will make me whole.

No one can.
You took away my heart, my trust-
My scene of reason,

My belief in the power of love,
To heal the heart-
Is broken-

But I must find away.
I must go on living.
I must love again.

I must reach beyond the crowed.
Find that new face to adore.
Let the wind whisper new loves for me.

Reach beyond the madness- the sorrow- the well of grief.
Find that place inside myself that loves Me.
Heal.

There is a hole inside my heart.
A fertile garden bed where love can grow,
And blossom.

And someday soon,
I will plant a new rose, in my garden.
I will water it genteelly, and watch it grow.

Ann T. Fenelon
11-25-01

A Villanelle To Love: A Rainbow Dream

Last night, I dreamed, your heart called out my name.
I awakened to find, that you were merely a phantom love.
My love for you is like a mired rainbows hue.

You speak to me of loves deepest, hopes, and desires.
Can't you see the flames of my soul's true desire?
Last night, I dreamed, your heart called out my name.

If you look into my eyes, you'll see my soul on fire.
If you listen, with your heart, my soul will speak its desire.
My love for you is like a mired rainbows hue.

You look at me, and through me, but you really don't see.
How can you be so blind to the love standing right before you?
Last night, I dreamed, your heart called out my name.

You try to reason, your love for me away, with logic.
But love, cannot be reasoned away, with nonsensical thinking.
My love for you is like a mired rainbows hue.

Surrender, to the love your heart must be feeling.
Let me touch you soul to mine, and fill you heart with dreams.
Last night, I dreamed, your heart called out my name.
My love for you is a mired rainbows hue.

Ann T. Fenelon
11-15-01

Angry Words

Words that cut to the heart,
Fast and quick-
Blunt and true.
Angry words meant
To hurt the soul.

Spoken out of spite.
Staple pain on the heart.
Cannot be forgotten.
Time does not heal all.
Keep your tongue

To save a tender heart.
Walk away.
Think before you speak.
Once anger enters the
Universe,

It gives birth to hate.
Killer of love.
Breeder of discontent.
Free your tongue of anger.
Speak only with your heart.

Ann T. Fenelon
1-11-02

Believe In Me

Hold on to me and believe.
In our love and the magic we create.
Believe in me as I believe in you.
In times of adversity we need to hold on to each other.
But instead we let voices of ill content pull us apart.

People who do not wish us well.
People who take pleasure in seeing us separated.
People whose homes are less the ideal, find ours lacking.
People who want you and some who want me to be alone,
People who will break apart our happy home,

And destroy the love we have worked so hard to build.
Love takes time and work to build a lasting stronghold.
We have put the work in, let us rep the benefits,
This enduring prize is our reward, for time well spent.
Hold fast to me, and love me as I love you,

Let nothing separate us.
People, who seek to destroy us,
Well perish in their jealousies.
The love we have built can never be destroyed.
If we just believe in each ours love.

Ann T. Fenelon
12-12-01

Coming Down From The Mountain

When Moses came down with the tablets,
He must have forgotten the commandment get even.
But it had to be one.
Cause mankind has no trouble following it.
We're out for blood every chance we get.

And not just the big things like 9-11.
That day gives emergency 911 a whole new meaning.
But the little things that can take us beyond reason.
Like some Joe Doe bumps you on the street.
And your ready to take his head off.

But he gives you that F WITH ME LOOK!!!
And you back off.
Inside your gut it eats you away.
Building to the point of boil and you blow.
And the authorities pull what's left of the next JOE DOE.

Off the tracks at 59th Street,
They had to stop the A all day.
This poor guy from Queens,
His crime, he spilled coffee on you.
That is one hell of a wake up call.

But now that I think of it GET EVER,
Was not a commandment.
It is a man made remedy for what ails you.
"Moses never brought that down no mountain."
But maybe we should all put it in a deep-deep hold.

Ann T. Fenelon
12-22-01

Climbing Out

You find yourself in a well
Of depression.
Fight to climb out.
Each day you sink deeper.
Rain clouds move in.
Stormy season has come.

You try to remember;
The last time you smiled.
The last time you wanted to.
Stop watching the news,
Long ago.
Makes you even more miserable.

Hold on to hope;
Says the voice inside your head.
Hope is gone.
I gave that up last year.
Right along with faith.
It was the charitable thing to do.

A noble act; my last.
So I try the climb again.
Reach for the top;
Find a pocket of strength.
Hidden deep inside myself.
Hold on to just one more day.

Live to fight one more day.
Do battle with the dragon.
Look the demon in the eyes.
Fight for air;
Breathe a breath for life.
Reclaim, my faith look for hope.

Ann T. Fenelon
2-08-02

Come To My Heart

His is an invitation, a gift of love.
He gave this gift to all.
With arms open wide he died.

A simple man with a simple message, LOVE.
"Come to my heart if you have a heavy load,
And I will give you rest."

In the world today was his sacrifice in vain.
We disregard human life.
Kill one another in the blink of an eye.

Turn our backs and ignore the suffering of humankind.
Are we worthy of his gift?
Are we deserving of his sacrifice of love?

The answer is no.
We have turned his gift into a travesty.
But his gift is also a gift of hope.

And where hope lives all things become real.
And we can renew and honor his sacrifice.
By removing hate from our hearts.

And loving each other in his name.
So come to my heart, he lives there.
And bring your heart to mine.

Ann T. Fenelon
12-24-01

Call Of The Wild

There is a place in side myself.
That speaks to the underbelly of life.
Giving into this base vice,
I open my soul to its hidden desires.

Put on black leather,
And head down town.
The nightlife of New York,
Calls out my name,

I come alive.
Vampire of the night-
I flirt with the unknown.
A vagabond in need of pleasure-

I seek out,
Music, dance, bright lights,
And blue smoke,
Fill my veins with new blood.

Sustenance,
For the true Vampire of the night,
The Bar-Hopper-
I live for the call of the wild.

Ann T. Fenelon
1-18-02

What pain.
What sorrow.
Filled you heart that night.
What made you put the gun to your head.
At sixteen-

I search my heart trying to imagine your pain.
How abandoned you must have felt.
I cry bitter tears for you.
If only I would have had the chance to say-
I love you-I care about what happens to you.

But you didn't give me a chance.
You didn't give yourself a chance.
I'm not judging you.
I'm just trying to make sense of something,
That makes no sense at all.

You were sixteen years old.
You had your whole life ahead of you.
No momentary pain or sorrow justifies,
The permanent solution of death,
Not when you're sixteen.

Hell not even when you're sixty.
But you're gone.
You're DIED.
And no philosophy changes that.
At sixteen-

So I stand at your grave.
And tell the other numb faces;
How much you were loved, and
How much you'll be missed.
I don't cry, I don't have anymore tears.

But I scream inside.
To God- the universe- are to who ever the hell-
Caused you pain.
And put that gun in your hand.
At sixteen-

Ann T. Fenelon
11-27-01

A woman's love

Is more valuable then gold,
More precious then diamond
Or pearl,
Immeasurable in its worth;

Brings a man to his knees,
And a lady to tears,
Yearning to have a woman's love,
Needing to be loved,

This is the power of a woman's love.
Melts your heart, and burns your soul.
Numbs the brain, have you taking-
To yourself-

Out walking the streets at night,
Afraid to go home alone,
Afraid to sleep alone,
Without a woman's love-

Life is not worth living.
The future holds no hope.
The day has no sun.
The night has no stars or moon.

Without a woman's love-

A. T. F.
11-20-01

A Wink And A Smile

Tell me again-
How much you love me.
That my trust in you
Is justified,
And our love is right.

Your sugar-sweet smile,
Takes me to a place,
Where reason dissolves into lust
And I stop listing,
To the doubting devil.

He's not on my
Shoulder by invitation.
But, rather a product of
Doubt.
I think he likes

The ride.
But there's that
Smile again.
Makes my mouth
Water.

Just a wink and
A smile I'm yours.
No doubt,
In my mind.
When you smile that, smile its love.

Ann T. Fenelon
1-10-02

Dream Weaver

You came to my door.
With a handful of stars,
The moon in your pocket,
And love only for me.

You lied.
Syrupy words pour out your mouth.
Stardust kisses fell like rain.
You told the sun to rise.

And it did.
Every word-
Every kiss-
Was magic,

You made me love you.
Then like all good magician.
You upped and disappeared.
Days and weeks,

No sweet kisses.
No magic words of love,
To fill my head and
Move my heart.

Two months later,
I still don't know,
If you were real.
Or, what I did to make you go.

One magical summer
And no regrets.
Special assistant,
To the magician of love.

You made the moon stand still.
Filled my nights,
With stardust kisses.
And life was magic for a while.

Ann T. Fenelon
1-12-02

Contempating Spring

Clouds like painted silk;
Float by on a sea blue sky.
Can spring be far behind?
I stroll in the lazy winter sun.
No artist brush could capture;
The beauty of this sight.

The trees will blossom
Into life.
Birds will sing.
Flowers burst into color.
Lovers walking hand in hand,
The magic of spring begins.

Bees buzzing from flower
To flower ignite fragrance
In the air.
All the world steps away
From their winter coats.
Spring reclaims her throne.

Ann T. Fenelon
2-10-02

Dream Lover

You come to me
Between the hours
Of night and day,

To break old taboos:
Of Black and White-
To lay with me,

We found: Your hard white skin,
        To my soft black-

We meld: An Iron Brown.

We part: Your soft Tan skin.
        From my Hard-Hard,
Brown-

A.T.F.
11-24-01

Could This Be Love

When I see you
I feel weak-
In the pit of my
Stomach,
Could this be love?

Or just the flu-
Feels like the flu.
I get hot all over,
And dizzy.
My heart beats fast,

And I start to see-
Stars; they dance.
And I hear music-
Hum for no good,
Reason at all.

Smiling-
Look I'm doing it now.
Laughing-
It's really silly.
A grown woman-

Acting like a school
Girl-
Really this just can't
Be happening-
Not to me.

Love-
It just can't be.
The flu-
The only answer-
Possible-

But here I go again.
Smiling-
Laughing-
Humming-
And there's that music.

Get a hold of yourself.
You're a reasonably-
Intelligent-
Person-
Analyze this properly.

Smiling for no reason-
This is LOVE!
Laughing for no reason-
This is LOVE!
And humming-

This is certainly,
LOVE-
This is LOVE.
I'm in LOVE.
I LOVE YOU.

A.T.F.
11-14-01

Cuts Like A Knife

My head still can't get around your leaving.
And it cut like a knife in my heart.
The pain of losing you is unreal.
The thing that really hurts is not knowing why you left.
Just to come home and find you gone.

Did it get to good between us and you had to run.
That's your m.o. love hard and leave before you get left.
DID I DO SOMETHING TO HURT YOU?
Did I love you to much or not enough?
For the life of me I don't know what.

I opened my heart to you and took you in.
And gave you safe harbor from the storm of life,
A place where you could be yourself,
But chaos is the air you breathe.
And chaos chokes me to death.

But I would have lived in chaos gladly.
Just to see your smile every morning.
You're gone now and my heart is in chaos.
And it cuts like a knife and leaves me numb.
But I can breathe again, and life holds hope.

I hope you fine yourself.
Before you can really love someone you have to know yourself.
And I hope I will find someone to love without all the baggage.
We both deserve a chance at happiness.
We couldn't find it with each other.

But that does not mean that we are undeserving of love.
It just means that we need to keep on looking.
What ever it was that made you leave.
Was something I could not give you.
For that I'm sorry.

And you leaving without explanation I can forgive.
What hurt was not being given the chance to make things right.
That still stings to the core.
But loving someone means forgiving them.
And I will always love you.

Ann T. Fenelon
12-16-01

Contemplation Of The Unknown

It is the fear of the Unknown,
That lives in the hearts of men;
This rules our souls,
And breaks our reason,
To spill the blood of all mankind,
And in doing so we slap the face-
Of GOD.

The giver of reason, and free-
Will.
It becomes so easy to hate.
To punish-
To kill-
To destroy-
Without reason or consequence-

And the question then becomes-
Where is GOD?
Does he see-
Does he known-
Does he care-
Does he really exist?
And if so were?

A.T.F.
11-12-01

Dream Walker

You come at night with a silken sack of dreams.
You spin a web of mystical adventure.
Your gift is the journey.

Magical rainbow dancer,
Weave for me a midnight song of love.
Hold out you hand in invitation;

I will gladly follow your lead.
Dance with me, on clouds of white and gold.
Let the hue of the sun melt into the mist of the moon.

Of silver and gold,
Are the colors of this midnight dream.
You have traveled so far.

And now you hold me near your heart.
All day have I longed to be held by you.
All night have I waited for this moment.

To know you in my dream,
To have you sing to me of love.
To surrender all of my heart to you,

In this dream journey,
To paradise, I will love you always.
Morning comes much too soon.

First light leaves me longing for your touch.
The warmth of your hands,
On my back, as we dance, stays in my heart.

All day I think of you;
And hope the night will bring you near to me.
My sweet Dream Walker, will you dance with me tonight.

Ann T. Fenelon
12-10-01

Dream Of The Heart

In the mist of a dream, you come to me.
You whisper words my heart longs to hear.
But I am unable to grasp their meaning.
Frustrated by this I fight the need for sleep.
It comes and with it, you return.
You face is more defined.
The shape is soft and your lips are full and round.
I imagine your kiss.

When you speak to me your words, I comprehend.
For weeks now, I have imagined this moment.
The touch of your hand, the warmth of your kiss,
And the way I would fit in your arms.
When you love me, the confines of my dream dissolve.
You are real to me and then I wake.

Frustrated, angry, and alone I wake with a feeling of loss.
With all your promises of eternal love,
You have abandon my.
I sleep but do not dream.
Thinking only of your kisses, I live my life in a haze.
Day in and day out, I curse the night,
Because I know, you will not come to me.

There you are standing before me.
I know this is not a dream some horrid aberration.
The sun is to hot to be night.
I am standing up, not lying down.
But it's your face, and when you speak to me, your voice.
I pinch my cheek and return you smile.

****

We are lovers now.
And I smile each time you tell me.
How well we fit together.
Like we have known each other always,
And loving me comes so naturally to you.

That all your dreams of love are coming true,
And that day at the vegetable stand was such good luck.
How you never shop there.
I kiss you and agree.
I decide not to tell you about my dreams.
And let you think the coincidence is the reason;
We fit so well together.

Besides, I find it hard sometimes to believe.
That you are a dream of my heart come true.
I had a dream about the love of my life.
And when I saw your face,
I knew my dream had come true.

Ann T. Fenelon
12-26-01

Confusion

Disorder in the ranks,
Mass confusion on the ground,
Love bomb dropped;
In lap, more lust to come.

What do you mean?
You love me?
Last time we conversed.
You expressed-

You're extreme distaste,
For me and the love I had for you.
Could it be that-
I'm in a relationship now.

And you heart felt desire,
Is nothing more then:
I don't want you and-
I don't want you with anyone.

So my natural response,
To your offer of unending love-
Is simple-
Much too little, much-much too late-

And as I walk away,
I think, does love, always have to play its game.
Can it just be open and honest.
And then I think, I have that now-

This is way I can walk away.

A.T.F.
11-22-01

Coming Down Like Rain

Trouble falls like rain.
Hard and frequent,
Like a winter storm;
Down south.
Freezing cold;
Cuts, to the bone.
White-hot pain.
Anesthetize the body.
Keeps your life in limbo,
Waiting for the next
Shoe to drop,
And it always does.
No need to ask God
Why me!
You already know.
It can only be SINS,
Of a past life.
I had to have killed someone.
Someone very important,
Cause I keep paying for it
Over and over and over again,
Once I walk out of one mess.
Here comes Mister.
I'm down for the count.
What don't kill you,
Makes you.
That's the lie
We buy.
To keep on living,
And the trouble keeps falling like rain.

Ann T. Fenelon
1-29-02

HEART AND SOUL

YOU LIVE IN THE SOUL
OF ME-
RIGHT IN THE HEART OF ME-
YOU ARE MY LIFE.

MY REASON-
MY PREAYER-
MY BREATH-
MY LIGHT-

ALL THAT YOU ARE TO ME-
ALL THAT YOU CAN EVER BE-
ALL THAT GIVES LIFE TO ME-
IS WHAT YOU ARE TO ME?

MY HEART AND SOUL,
MY LOVER AND WIFE,
MY GIVER OF ALL THINGS GOOD,
THIS IS WHO YOU ARE TO ME.

A.T.F.
11-8-01

En Mitad De La Noche

In the middle of the night,
When I'm all alone in my bed-
I pray-
You come to me.

With star light moons-
In your eyes;
With whispers of haven's
Sweet refrain.

Sweet melodies so soft
And fine.
Then take me gently,
In your arms-

With promises of Paradise;
Right here on earth.
Heavenly-Sweet-Angel,
Please stay with me.

Until the morning's light,
Then take me home to your-
Paradise.
En Mitad De La Noche-
En Mitad De La Noche-
En Mitad De La Noche-

A.T.F.
11-10-01

First Date

You say I'll call and you don't.
I hate to go on blind dates.
They end badly every time.

You make the investment.
Take the time to dress up.
Say and do the right things.

Hold your breath, the whole night.
Somehow, you still manage to screw up.
Wait for the phone to ring,

And replay the entire evening.
Was it something I said or didn't say?
You were beautiful, and I was nerves.

After three day's, the phone rings.
You've been out of town on business.
Enjoyed our first date and would like to see me.

Tonight-
Tomorrow night.
You could come over right now.

And you do with Yellow Roses.
My favorite, mentioned it once at dinner.
You remembered.

Three days late and right on time,
And all I do is smile.
"How was your trip?"

Ann T. Fenelon
12-30-01

First Snow

Cold and brisk-
Blinding white-
Winters true intent.

To chill the night,
Make the day soft, quiet.

The warmth that precedes,
Lets me know you have return.

Quaint in beauty,
Pliable to the touch,
You are all seasons crowning glory.

Snow men-
Snow angels-
Snow balls to fight.

Await your return.
Fluffy snow flicks,
Fill the night.

Blanket the day.
In white pillow hills,
And freeze time.

Ann T. Fenelon
12-27-01

Flirtation

It starts with the eyes.
Subtle,
Nuance takes over.
Shy smiling eyes;
Penetrate
The heart
Of your soul.

You look away.
A shy smile
Of your own.
The dance begins.
I see you,
Do you see me?

A shy laugh,
For good measure.
Then, direct
Penetration.
The lingering
Gaze;
Of intent.

Then,
The question becomes.
Who crosses the room?
Deep breathe-
For confidence.
I make my move.

Ann T. Fenelon
1-25-02

Forgotten Shadows

In the mist of sorrow
I see your face.
Not quite clear,
At first,
Then you speak my name.

I know then that it's you.
Not a dream-
You're real to me.
Your eyes,
Your smile,
Your face,
Like an angel in white;
You've come.

Always,
When I need you.
Your there,
Like a bright light,
To guide me.

Before, I slip away.
On some melancholy
Journey,
Into the darkness of my soul.

Oh mama, hold me again.
Make things right.
Let me cry like a baby
In your arms

Tell me that I'm
A good person.
Worthy, of love.
Capable,
Of achieving happiness.

Let me be your baby.
Just for a little while.
Hold me till I sleep.
Help me dream,
Only happy dreams.

I miss you.
Your advice.
Your comfort.
Your love.

When I was a little girl;
You could fix anything.
Even in this surreal
Moment.
You've help me pull
Back,
From this darkness.

Your love carries me through.
Tomorrow,
Promises hope.
When my soul is drowning,
In forgotten shadows.
Only your love can save me.

Ann T. Fenelon
1-23-02

En Mitad De La Noche

In the middle of the night,
When I'm all alone
In my bed,
You come to me.

With moon light stars,
And Angel's wings-
To whisper-
Loves sweet refrain,

Sing for me sweet
Angel.
Melodies of heaven's
Paradise here on earth,

And hold me in your
Arms, until the morning
Light.
Then take me up to your,

Paradise.
En Mitad De La Noche-
En Mitad De La Noche-
En Mitad De La Noche-

A.T.F.
11-10-01

Fresh Start

New beginning-
New hope comes with a New Year.
Do the problems of the old disappear?
At the stroke of midnight,
A magic wand makes all things new.

There is no magic.
We simply fool ourselves.
Or, is it that we choose to believe?
In the possibility of hope,
And the inevitability of change,

That makes live real.
No soap opera dream.
No, make believe.
Just real and honest drama,
That makes life the journey;

We take day after day.
And year after year,
We choose to take the trip again.
So when the clock strikes 12.
May old acquaintances be forgot.

Ann T. Fenelon
1-01-02

Fragile

Your heart so easily broken
By unkind works,
Like an egg in rough hands.
I walk slowly around harsh
Subjects.

Reach inside with a gentle touch.
Trying not to revisit old hurts.
You put up wall so quickly.
I'm not the enemy at your gate.
I love you remember me.

We're in this together.
Isn't that the way love works.
We do it together or not at all.
If you shut down on me;
We lose everything.

I waited so long;
To have love in my life.
I can't let go so easily.
I have to fight for you and me.
Show me my fight is not in vain.

Let me in your fragile heart.
Tear down the walls.
I can't live out side your gate.
I won't live with half a love.
My heart is too fragile.

Ann T. Fenelon
2-09-02

Holding On

I once though the most important thing
In life was holding on to you.
But I now know that is just not true.
Letting go is the most important.

Letting you go and holding on to me,
Is the only thing that makes any sense.
This is the only way I can gain my sanity.
I lost my mind when I fell in love with you.

All sense of reason went walking out the door.
Go to bed at night and can't sleep.
Spend money on you I just don't have.
Cut off all my relationships with good friends.

I find that I'm lying to myself about you.
And the part that's really hard to believe,
Is that I am buying the lie.
No more!

Baby I got to let you go.
Cause, baby this love is killing me.
And I can do BAD by my dame self.
So you can hold on to yourself and I'll hold on to me.

Ann T. Fenelon
12-19-01

Home For The Holidays

Its time to make merry again,
Deck the halls and all that.
And lose sight of the real reason for the season.

We get caught up in the food and the presents.
We need to go down on our knees and pray.
Everyday should be a holiday.

In fact, it is so strange to me that kindness is seasonal.
That we run to church to pray for peace and love.
On this Holy-Holiday, when love for all mankind is propagated.

And the rest of the year we walk by and over the homeless.
The poor and disenfranchise people of society.
Do they not deserve a more compassionate world?

One in which everyday the possibility of hope can exist.
Our helping hand should be open 365 days a year not just one.
Let us make everyday a holiday.

And the gift we give is an open heart.
Celebrate life to the fullest.
And remember that J.C. is the only reason for the season.

24-7-365.
happy holiday.
Merry Xmas.

Ann T. Fenelon
12-15-01

Infatuation

Captured,
By the look in your eyes,
I surrender.
Agree to just one dance.
Nothing slow,
I need distance.
A buffer,
My heart is still tender.
I have to shield
My emotions.

So cavalier,
Is your intent.
I blush,
As I take hand.
Not quite ready,
To accept,
The nuances
Of your smile.

Steps away,
From the dance floor
The music slows.
I stop.
Taking my hand from yours.
As I start to turn,
You imprison me.
Putting your arms around
My waist.

The feeling,
So natural.
We slow-dance,
On the edge
Of the crowded floor.
Two-three-four,
Songs later;
I'm at your table.
Melting, into your smile.
Ready to accept your next invitation.

Ann T. Fenelon
1-24-02

Just Like Old Times

Seeing you,
Is just like old times.
Butter still melts in your mouth.
Lies rolling off your tongue
Like thunder,
Just like some used car hack.

Got me looking for the exit
And the lightening to hit
Your lying ass.
And after you tell me for the
Third, time how much you've
Changed.

I'm looking for the waiter,
And asking for the check.
This is one bridge I'll
Never cross again.
You had me paying rent.
On Big White Lies,

I could never live in.
So I just smile.
Tell you how good you look.
But, I really can't stay
Taking your number, I promise to call.
Then, hand it off to the waiter, with a tip and a smile.

Ann T. Fenelon
1-05-02

Just Today

I though about you again,
And called just to hear your voice-
On the machine,
A new message, answered me.

"I'm not home, leave your number."

No more US or We.
Painful-
Hard to hear your voice-
I did not leave my number.

I remember when we bought that machine.
We recorded our first message, together.

"We may be home, but we can't pick up."

****

Just today, there were five hang-ups on my machine.
I know it was you.
So I call your machine.
I hate your message.

"It's me, if your home please pick-up."
"Ok, here it goes, I love you-miss you-please come home."
"Ok, your not home."
"Please, give me a call."

"No I'm here!"
"Don't hang-up."
"Hi!"

****

Just today, we put a new message on our answering
machine.

"We are home, were not picking up, and we may never-
Ever-
Call you back."

****

Just today, I awaken to find you in my arms.
The phone rang and we didn't pick-up.
Around 2pm. We turned the ringer off.
Just for today.

Ann T. Fenelon
11-29-01

Longing

I find myself longing for you touch.
The way you hold me close early in the morning,
And kiss me softly until I wake.
Then you smile that little smile that tells me,
You're in the mood and ready.

Your eyes give you away every time.
You try to pretend that you'll be late for work.
When we both know that work is the last thing on your mind,
And you would call in sick in a heart beat.
So we kiss and make plans for the weekend.

We're in the middle of the sweet spot.
When the alarm goes off,
And we both know the weekend will be starting early.
Later in the shower, we practice our best flu voice.
Then we pack and head out for the beach.

We are both tired from the long drive.
So we go to the Inn for dinner.
When we get back to the beach house we build a warm fire.
And pick up were we left off that morning.
The next day we take a long walk on the beach.

Sunday evening the ride back to the city was quiet.
We were both replaying the special moments.
We hold hands the whole way home.
We can't wait until we can really touch.
I look deeply into you eyes and see just how you're longing.

Ann T. Fenelon
12-20-01

Looking For You

I sit all alone in the park.
And I look for you.
I try to see you on the faces of strangers.
Could she be you?
Are maybe, that little girl is she the one.
She would be the right age.
I imagine your smile.
I like to think about you in the park at play.
I carried you for nine months.
I loved you.
I still do.
Giving you a better life,
Is what I felt I had to do.

The people who took you were kind.
I know that they will be so good to you.
But I still think sometimes how it would be to hold you.
And kiss you good night.
Walk you to school.
Try and help you with home work too.

Today is your birthday and I got you a gift.
I do this each year.
Maybe someday, you'll look for me.
And I'll have them for you.

Happy birthday sweet baby,
Mama loves you.

Ann T. Fenelon
12-17-01

Looks Like Rain

The sky an angry-gray
Wash of light.
Hangs like a pall.

Distilling my contentment,
Like the rain, it holds.
A down pouring of sadness,
My tears fall as rain.

This depression is momentary.
It changes like the whims of weather.
Gloomy one moment-
Sunny the next-
Can one's heart live in such turmoil?

I dress warmly and take a walk.
Recalling, that the lack of sun,
In Winter is cause for depression.

Cool-crisp air fills my lungs.
Lift my spirits.
I look up through a cloud opening.
And catch a small patch of blue.

I begin to remember my love for Winter.
Knowing my prediction of rain was mistaken.
I head to the long trail along the lake.

Ann T. Fenelon
1-15-02

Little Baby

She comes to me at night.
Knocks on the door,
Waits for me to let her in,

I return to my place on the sofa.
I beckon her to me, with my hand.
She comes to me.

Sits down next to me,
And lays her head on my lap;
We begin our evening ritual.

I stroke her long silky hair.
Its radiant colors dance in the soft light.
Seconds- into minutes- into hours pass.

Without warning, she is up and at the door.
Her cool green eyes, now beckon to me.
For completion of our evening ritual,

I stand, the door opens;
And I watch, as she walks out,
Bravely into the night.

Ann T. Fenelon
11-23-01

Keeping The Faith

Holding on to love
Like some needful prayer
To God is all I can do.

But, each day little by little
You slip away from me.
First, you voice.

I could sit for hours
Listening to the sound
Of your voice.

That's gone now.
I can't see your eyes.
I remember they were brown.

But, what shade, what shape
I just can't recall.
A thousand times

I've gazed into them.
They've simply disappeared.
Oh, your sweet mouth,

I've kissed and kissed
All through the night.
Gone with the beauty

Of your face.
Slowly evaporated,
From my memory.

I fear my soul will
Lose you next.
But, I hold on like a prayer.

Then, some miracle
Takes place inside my heart.
Your beauty grows,

Right inside my heart.
The lithe softness of your face.
The sweet twinkle of your eyes.

The plush fullness of your lips.
All living inside my heart.
Just like a prayer.

Ann T. Fenelon
2-06-02

Lost

Out on your own in the desert of life,
You take comfort where you find it.
In the hand of strangers, you my find bread to eat.

Life so often leaves a brave heart cold and alone.
And a stranger is the only peace ones soul can hope for.
For a simile, a kind word, even a warm bed to rest in.

You make the chose to surrender yourself.
For just one night of human contact,
You sell you soul.

And take pleasure, in the momentary warmth of skin-to-skin.
In the eyes of a stranger, you see yourself as whole.
But the moment ends and the stranger is gone.

And you find yourself more lost then before.
Out in the desert, in search for the next kind face,
And warm hands, to erase the stigma of what has passed.

But nothing can or ever will.
And lost in the desert of life is all you will ever be.
Except for the rain, that onslaught which purifies,

The desert and sets all wrongs right.
Salvation comes to the desert, in the form of a rainbow.
A covenant of salvation from God, the giver of hope,

Goodness and peace.
But we so often refuse to reach for that out stitched hand.
Instead we continue to suffer in our own condemnation.

Lost in the desert of self imposed exile,
Content to reach for a stranger,
Instead of healing the broken spirit we have become.

Reach instead for the only oasis this desert holds.
Love of self.
Forgive yourself, look to the horizon and walk out of this desert.

Ann T. Fenelon
12-11-01

Love As A Portrait

Your face-
As clear to me-
As an Ansel Adams,
Landscape
Painted on my mind,
It moves through my soul.

Like a beautiful-
Tropical bird,
All colors
On display
Singing out its love,
You move through my soul.

The warmth-
Of your body,
As we touch
Fills my heart with emotion,
I cry.
You move my soul.

I give way.
Surrender.
Your face-
Your touch-
Carry me to paradise.
Claim my soul.

Ann T. Fenelon
1-03-02

Love Like Rain

You make my love come down
Like rain on a hot sunny day.
Scorching the black hot pavement.
Sizzling heat rising.

My steam surrounds you.
Intoxicated by my wine
You drink your fill.
Leaving me spent.

Slowly the thunder builds
In me once more.
You move close to the well
Your thrust for my evident,

In your eyes.
I open to your need
Secure in my ability to please
I release the storm within.

We dance naked in the rain.
Drink often from the wells
Of life.
Drift away with the rain.

Ann T. Fenelon
2-25-02

Love Is A Formula

Holding on to the familiar,
Like a baby clinging,
To its mother is what we do.
Human nature, upholds
Our instincts.
To adhere,
To maintain the status quo.

I love you and you love me.
Simple equation.
The formula works.
X times Y equals Z.
We hold on
To this basic truth.

Letting go would signify,
That life does not work
On script.
The unknown always
Steps in.
When love turns into,
"I care deeply for you".

X times,
I care deeply for you,
Does not equal Z.
No need to acknowledge
Failure.
And letting go-
Hell,

You're already gone.
And I'm left,
Holding the love.
But, the formula does work.
This much is true.
You're just the wrong Y,
For my X.

So I let go.
Reformulate.
Search,
For a new mathematical participant.
Enthusiastically,
Researching all viable candidates.
{I love you and you love me},
{X times Y equals Z},
I will prove this equation true.

Ann T. Fenelon
1-30-02

Love Bugs

I have two love bugs.
They are magnets,
That I keep at the top
Of the refrigerator,
They make me smile.

When I look at them,
I think of us.
Kissing-
Laughing-
Talking- about our,

Love and life together;
Making plans for the
Future. Our hopes
And dreams, plans
And scams-

Just being together.
In love like Love Bugs-
Do.
Kissing. Hugging.
Me---------You.

A.T.F.
11-09-01

Love Me Tender

Young Elvis hangs on my wall.
Guitar in hand,
Far away, look in his eyes.
Love Me Tender is what he will play.

I can almost hear him sing.
Think of you in my arms.
We dance all night.
And our love was so very tender.

Magic the way music can transport your soul.
In a smoke filled bar our eyes, meet.
Your touch, personal and casual,
Is the invitation I need.

"I love this song would you like to dance?"
"It's why I crossed the room."
Lost in the music and each another,
We feed quarters to the box all night.

Playing this song and fall in love,
We make Love Me Tender our song.
You gave me the plaque to week later.
We played our song and danced all night long.

Ann T. Fenelon
12-28-01

Her Face

The day I first saw your face
Love was all I could see.
There was no need to see
Beyond your sweet-sweet
Face.

When I wake even in my
Sleep-
Your sweet face is all I
See-
All I need see.

I plucked a lash from
Your face,
I keep in a locket
Near my heart-
Your sweet face is near my heart.

Someday in my arms you
Will stay;
And your sweet face will
Touch mine.
Sweet-face to sweet-face,

Love is only a matter of
Time-
Your sweet face next to
Mine.
I see only your face.

Ann T. Fenelon
11-05-01

Picnic In The Rain

Picnic basket packed.
Rain begins.
Must we cancel?
No!

Light fire.
Stay in.
Hold me close.
Start fire burning within.

Slow knowing hands.
Move.
Caress my hips and thighs.
Soft kisses between my breasts.

Discovering,
Epicurean delights.
No basket can hold.
The taste of curious wine,

Take from me your portion.
And I will have my fill.
My thirst for you has grown.
Later, we eat grapes and listen to the rain.

Ann T. Fenelon
1-04-02

Paint Me In Your Love

Your love unfolds
As a portrait.
You paint in soft
Pastels.
Your love for me
On the blank canvas,
Of my heart.

Every corner,
Of my heart
Holds the light
And shades
Of your vibrant creation.
Tender touches,
Soft shy kisses,
Your love transforms me.

Each day you open me
To new spaces,
Inside my heart.
Where love can grow.
It's only through
The artistry of your touch.
That I live as love.
I exist as a portrait
Of your love.

Ann T. Fenelon
1-31-02

Love On The Line

Our love is on the line.
We need to make it our top priority.
Love needs work, and time to grow.

We take each other for granted.
We hold on to anger.
We refuse forgiveness, and compromise.

How much longer can we go on?
If we don't communicate we die.
Our love will die from stagnation.

Love is like water, it must flow.
It must keep moving, to the river of our souls.
Talk with me, flow with me, and help our love grow.

You show more compassion to a stranger.
You spend more time on a grocery list, then on me.
Is this relationship really important to you?

Am I important to you?
Is our love your main priority?
Do we have a future?

Hole me close to you heart.
Open you heart to me.
Let's make our love work.

Let's talk like we did when we first got together.
Let's take long walks on the beach.
Let us hold hands, and make wishes on stars.

Open-up to me again,
Trust in you heart.
Trust in me.

I won't let you down.
Reach out for me.
I'm right here, I won't go away.

Our love is real.
Our love is here to stay.
Our love is on the line.

Ann T. Fenelon
12-03-01

Procrastination

I needed to tell you to go to hell three weeks ago.
I put it off.
So go to hell.
Live in hell.
Die in hell.
Stay in hell.

I needed to tell you that I loved you three weeks ago.
I put it off.
So go to hell.
Live in hell.
Die in hell.
Stay in hell.

I needed to tell you I saw, with her three weeks ago.
I put it off, until today.
"Oh, your clothes are at Good Will."
"Oh, your car it's been repossessed."
"Oh, you got to get the hell up out of here."
"And stay in hell."

I needed to tell you, I never loved you.
But I put it off, until now.
"You're sorry and yo'mama sorry too."
"You're not even good in bed."
"And you look like hell."
"So go to HELL!"

"Live in HELL!"
"Die in HELL!"
"Stay in HELL!"
I will never put off doing what I need to do again.
You sleep deeper, and dream better at night.
Never put off for three weeks, what you could do today.

Ann T. Fenelon
12-04-01

Purple Fusion

Electric magic swirling on the dance floor,
You and I locked in loves embrace.
To star-crossed lovers,
Taking one last chance,
On happiness-

The everlasting kind,
The stuff they write songs about.
Like the song playing-
In my head, while we dance.
"Will you still love me tomorrow?"

"Will you!"
"What?"
"Will you love me tomorrow, and the next day and
the next?"
"I love you right here, right now, let tomorrow take
care of itself."

And I smile, look into your eyes, pull you close,
And lose myself-
In you-
In the music-
And the PURPLE FUSION HAZY-

ANN T. FENELON
11-19-01

Rain

Falling water-
Cool and moist
Heaven's reward,
The earth receives as blessing.

Hot-Summers release.
Springtimes promise.
Winter's curse,
It freezes natures will.

On a beach by the Ocean,
It helps to cleanse the mind.
In my room in my bed,
It draws you near to me.

At your grave,
On this hill,
It cries my pain for me.
Salty tears to melt my soul away.

Ann T. Fenelon
1-06-02

Rainy Day Blues

Slow drizzle,
You're going again.
On a trip to Austin,
A turquoise bracelet
Was my gift last year.

Its bluish-green hue
Reminds me of your eyes.
I only ware it in absents,
Of their beauty.
To feel close to you.

You touched
My ring finger;
Kissed me with a smile.
Before, you boarded
The plane.
I predict a bluish-green ring
In my future.

At home,
I look at the rain,
Through foggy windows.
Finger my bracelet,
Sent you sunshine in Austin.
Pray,
You back to my arms.

Ann T. Fenelon
1-21-02

Sail Away

On a blue-bright sea
Sun, hot and high
Seagulls flying by,
We have sailed away.

Salty mist fills my nostrils.
I inhale deeply open my lungs.
Pure air invigorates my spirit.
And I sail away,

On this gossamer sea.
Crisp-white sail
Stretches to the heavens.
To capture Neptune's prize

The wind.
That carries us away.
Out to sea.
Beyond the veiled horizon.

We escape the hold of land.
And submerge in indigo.
Become one with the sea.
As we sail away.

Ann T. Fenelon
1-08-02

Rude Awakening

You take me for granted.
Believe that I will always be their.
When you call,
Think again,

Think long and hard.
Do not assume I will drop everything for you.
I don't like being taken for granted.
I would never do such a thing to you.

So when you call me at the last minute.
I have other plans, and can't make it.
I have no plans.
I will not be taken for granted.

Respect me.
Or don't call me when you need baling out.
I don't need you in my life.
I do just fine on my own.

Do not presume to read my mine.
Ask me what I want and need.
I'm not afraid to tell you.
Maybe, you're not ready to hear.

Maybe, you're not ready for a rude awakening.
But, you can best believe,
I'm ready to give you one.
Believe me you won't see it coming.

But you will feel its effect.
The word NO!
A very small word,
That carries one hell of a punch.

A word that has taken me a long time to learn,
And an even longer time to say to you,
But I have mastered the art of NO.
Welcome to my world.

Ann T. Fenelon
12-06-01

Mon Petit Pêche

Warm to the touch soft and fuzzy.
With the sweetest smell of fresh honey,
It invites and entices me.
"Come take that first bite."

I haste wanting to experience its entire splendor,
The anticipation is half the pleasure.
I rub her sweet softness on my cheek.
Kiss her warm sweet fuzzy flesh.

That first bite is the true test.
Will she live up to my expectation?
Will I suffer disappointment?
Will she abandon me after such a warm invitation?

I slowly sink my teeth into her succulent flesh.
Her ripe flesh explodes filling my mouth with flavor.
Her rich juices drip from my tongue to my lips.
And her kiss is sweet and wet and satisfying.

I hungrily devour her pungent meaty flesh.
Her spices invade my entire body.
Until all that remains, is the pit.
Needing to possess all of her,

I pop the pit into my greedy mouth.
Biting hard I split the pit in half.
Freeing the almond shaped seed.
I hold the seed in one hand.

And the two halves of the pit,
I abandon to the ground.
They bake in the rays of the sun.
I watch as the last drop of moister evaporates.

I pop the seed into my mouth.
And roll it around with my tongue.
I bite the tart treat.
And walk away completely satisfied.

Ann T. Fenelon
12-23-01

Needful Things

Like some injured bird
You huddle near me.
Quivering,
In a pale pink gown,
In need of love.

Can my love save you?
Is it enough to heal your soul?
Quiet,
The nagging question
That lives in your heart.

Am I worthy?
Deserving of your love.
Deserving of happiness.
At peace with the choices,
I've made.

Holding you.
Your question becomes mine.
Taking on the weight
Of your heartache
Bewilders me.

We are both needful things.
Discovering love,
In a painful world.
Reach inside my heart
You'll find your own.

Ann T. Fenelon
1-27-02

Same Head Same Heart

I combed my mama's hair.
And I took notice of the shape and size of her head.
Then I compared her head to mine.
Same shape, smaller size.
Less brain capacity,
But we both had the same shape.

When I told her this,
She said she had shape mine like hers in the hospital.
"I would touch mine and then shape yours."
"With all my other children I never though to do that,
But with you it was such a natural thing to do."
I told her I was glad and proud to share her shape.

From then on she would touch my head and say,
"Same head, same heart always."
I believe this is what I hold on to now that she's gone.
When I was her baby she shaped my head and heart.
I know that she is always with me.
In the shape of my head and the beat of my heart she lives.

Ann T. Fenelon
12-18-01

Mirrored Pools

My reflection-
In your eyes
Is magical.

A transformation,
Of light and color.
I dance.

Waltz on beams,
Of azure and indigo.
Tango into orange-red.

Only in your eyes.
Can this magic exist.
Light and color become one.

Become me.
A rainbows hue.
Reflected in your eyes.
And magic still.
Light and color
Melt.

Into sound.
Into song.
I sing.

And my song,
The one I sing.
Is the song of love.

The love I have,
For you.
When I look, in you eyes.

Only in your eyes.
Do I dance.
Do I sing.

Ann T. Fenelon
1-05-02

Murky Waters

There's no black or white
When it comes to love.
The water is always murky.
You dive in head first,
At your own risk.

Over and over
You tend to swim,
In the deep end.
Hold your breath
Fight for love.

When the water is clear
I look in.
Seeing the bottom
Knowing the risk,
Holds no thrill.

In love, the unknown
Makes the chase
Worth the run.
In love, not seeing the bottom
Means you never reach it.

Ann T. Fenelon
2-04-02

New Year

Time to make merry again,
Move out to the new day.
The New Year has begun.

But what will this year bring?
War or peace----
Oil for the thief in our White House

And death for the innocent
Who must carry out his madness.
Happy Fing New Year---

GOD blesses America.
Happy New Year
God help us all.

Ann T. Fenelon
1-9-03

Of Loves Lament

I think it was you that said
Forever-
Was that just a lie?
Or did you really mean
Forever-
When you said it,
Was your heart in it?

My heart was.
I believed in every word;
Of your sweet promise of,
Forever-
I still do believe in you.
I need to believe in you, and
Forever-

But now you're gone,
And so is my
Forever-
You didn't have to say it,
I would love you anyway.
My arms are empty now,
And my bed is cold,
Forever-

A.T.F
11-11-01

Open Hands

Love comes with open hands.
Unconditional-
Freely given and freely taken.
Steady in motion.
Fluid in standing still,
Awaiting appreciation,

Love needs time to grow.
Slow and gentle hands caressing,
And embracing each moment of love.
Never grabbing.
Never hurried.
Passionate in its patience.

Tender in its release.
Joyous in its ability to surrender.
To crave.
To hunger.
To thirst.
Love for loves sake with open hands.

Ann T. Fenelon
11-26-01

Patriotism

I ordered a shower curtain from a catalog.
When the box came inside was an American flag.
The adhesive kind you put in windows.
I did just that.
Put it right in my kitchen window.
Like all the other God Blessing Americans.

I did not run out to buy a flag.
If it did not come to me in that box,
It would not be in my window.
On 4 July, I don't wave the flag either.
Nothing to prove,
I'm a damn "GOOD" American everyday.

I volunteer at my church;
Feed the homeless.
I give my money and myself.
Take time to give a little back,
For all I have been given.
It's what real Americans do.

I did not need two buildings come down to start.
And that fact will not make me stop.
Decency exists in all of US.
Sometimes, we have to look a little hard to find it.
And sometimes, we need a tragedy to remind US.
That united we stand, PATROITISM LIVES!!!

Ann T. Fenelon
1-02-02

Only Logical

The logical mind tries to reason,
With the impetuous heart.
To no end.

Matters of the heart
Have no logic.
Love is reason in itself.

The heart wants what it wants.
Moves the body into action.
And the mind silenced;

By the heart fights for voice.
Must ask the question why?
The hearts replay.

Is always Because.
Because I want.
Because I need.

Just Because.
Logic be damn,
I want what I want.

Some might call this lust.
I know that it is just the nature,
Of the heart.

Very simple.
And to the point.
It's only logical.

Ann T. Fenelon
1-13-02

Open Mind

I try to see the world
Through your eyes.
Empathize with your pain.
Walk in your shoes.
Keep an open mind.

It's hard to know what to say.
I respect your privacy.
Don't want to open old wombs.
You suffer in silence.
Refuse, to share your grief.

I watch you slowly drowning.
The sorrow is taking you under.
You think there is no way out.
I want to be your lifeline.
If you only open your heart to me.

My love is not pity.
Its open free of all judgment.
There's safety in numbers.
Lean on me just a little.
Trust me; I will never let you down.

Ann T. Fenelon
2-01-02

Sunset

At the end of the day,
We walk hand in hand,
Along the beach.
Looking to the horizon.
Watching the rainbow of colors;
Dance on the waters edge.
Listen, for the sizzle of the sun.
As it touches the blue-basin,
Of the sea.

Quietly, dissolving into twilight.
Swallowed whole by the sea.
As the purple, red, yellow,
And orange lights of last sun,
Melt into the
Canvas of night.
We stand in awe,
Discovering the evening star.
Slowly rising from the sea.

Ann T. Fenelon
2-03-02

Silence As Love

I wake early;
Listen in on the silence,
Of the house.
Watch you sleep.

Cooing,
Like a baby.
When you have a cold,
You snore.

Rough noise,
For such an angel
Face.
I keep C-tabs, on hand.
Hate to see you sick.

I kiss your cheek.
Inhale your soft warmth.
Reach-out to stop the clock.
Wake you with a kiss instead.

Smiling, you're good morning.
Taking me;
Kissing me to laughter.
The silence is broken.
The joy of our love,
Fills our home.

Ann T. Fenelon
1-22-02

Stillness

Motionless, I wait
For my heart to beat
Do I go on living?
Do I lie down and die?
I hear myself speak.
So I know that I'm alive.
I see people moving about.

I take that first breath.
Feel my heart pumping
Blood through my body.
But you're not so how can I be.
We were in the same car
Hit by the same truck.
I'm numb, can't cry.
I'm alive and empty.

When my mama died
I was empty.
It took three years
But you filled me up
Made me laugh again.
Now you're gone.
Who fill me up this time?
Who will make noise
In the stillness of my soul?

Ann T. Fenelon
2-12-02

Step Into The Night

SAID THE SPIDER TO THE FLY,
COME CLOSE TO ME,
AND LET ME WHISPER-
IN YOUR EAR.

LET ME TANGLE YOU IN MY
WEB AND SPIN YOU FABLES
OF LONG FORGOTTEN-
PLACES.

MAGICAL PLACES-
WHERE DREAMS COME-
TRUE.
LET ME TAKE YOU THERE.

HAVE NO FEAR MY FRIEND,
THERE'S SAFITY IN NUMBERS,
AND I'M YOUR WILLING-
GUIDE.

TAKE MY HAND-
WHAT LOVELY HANDS
YOU HAVE-
SLEEP-

WHAT LOVELY EYES
SLEEP-
AND LOVELY NECK
SLEEP-SLEEP-SLEEP-

A.T.F.
11-13-01

Snowbound

I love it when it snows.
Everything,
Frozen in white,
Still.

Its silent beauty
Opens my soul.
A quiet voice speaks
To my heart.

Reminding,
Me to slow down.
Take in a cool breathe.
Let go of stress.

Renew.
Winter, is my
Planting season.
My springtime.

Part bear,
I hibernate.
Contemplate.
Molt.

My metamorphosis,
Complete.
I wait on spring.
And harvest.

Ann T. Fenelon
1-19-02

Sunday Dreaming

It's Sunday and I'm daydreaming.
All about you,
And the love I'm felling.

Hearts singing, church bells ringing;
All because of you,
I'm in love with you.

Blue skies above, clouds roll by.
Blue birds flying high,
Singing as they pass us by,

Love is their lullaby.
Love is my anthems cry.
Love is our only joy.

Marry me on this Sunny-Sunday.
On this beautiful first day of May,
Will you marry me?

Happily in love we will be.
Sunday dreaming you and me,
If you say you'll marry me.

In love we'll be.
In love we'll stay.
If today is our wedding day.

Sunday dreaming for no reason,
If you say no to me,
My heart you'll be breaking.

Will you marry me?
Will you give me joy?
Will you love me?

Yes!
Yes!
Is what you're saying.

Your hand is what I'm taking.
My joy is what I'm claming.
True love is where I'm aiming.

Take my hand and say I do.
Walk me down the aisle.
Come Sunday Dreaming with me.

Ann T. Fenelon
12-02-01

Sickertized

Dear Patricia,

I find myself hobnobbing at local cafes.
Trying to expand my artistic predilections offering
one small glance into my subconscious mind, my art
has life and validation.

Love always
Ann
1-21-03

Sunday

The wind whips outside
My window.
Spilling cold air like rain.
I pull the covers over my
Head for warmth.
Look at my watch
Sleep.

Sunday is my lazy day.
Sleep late.
Have a long brunch
At the café.
Read the paper
Take care of little
Things around the house.

Make call and plans
For my week.
Go to a movie
Or, see a show.
Maybe go to the gym
Far a swim in the heated pool.

Stay in listen to Jazz.
Make dinner for you.
Buy the wine you like.
Or just stay in bed
With a good book.
Yeah! Sunday is my lazy day.

Ann T. Fenelon
2-11-02

Somewhere In Time

We have been here before.
You and I have loved before.
Somewhere in time-

You are my love, a love so familiar.
Tender and kind,
Warm and gentle,

You bring me home to myself.
You touch the soft center of my heart.
You fill my soul with peace.

When I look into your eyes-
I see myself as I truly am.
A simple woman in love,

With a beautiful lady, who loves me.
As I look deeper into your eyes-
I see my soul revealed.

And on it I find these simple words.
I love you Roxanne.
You are my friend-soul mate-lover-and wife.

We have always been this way.
We will always be this way.
Not now but somewhere in time.

Ann T. Fenelon
11-30-01

Things You Need To Know

Did you know that life has no set plan?
That it is determined by the work you put in.
And when we fail it's because we refuse to put in the work.

Sometimes though, the unexpected happenstance accrues.
And life leaves you no chose or way out.
And we are brought to a point of no return.

Where we make chooses that break our spirit.
We sell our soul and we take a road that leads to hell.
Be it material goods or physical pleasure.

But in the end all we are left with is SELF.
We have to be able to look in the mirror.
And respect the person looking back at you.

People come into our life to help or hinder us;
On our spiritual journey, we must discern if they
Wish us well or ill.

In the end we are held accountable for chooses made.
We can't point an accusing finger at anyone but ourselves.
We have to walk the walk and talk the talk.

Take responsibly.
"Life is what you make of it", is not just a cliché.
It's the truth.

Stand up make chooses and live with the consequences.
Don't be afraid to look in the mirror.
Know that the person looking back at you is SELF.

Your true self, the person you have built.
Through right chooses.
Good or bad the journey is in you own hands.

And at the end of the journey right or wrong you stand alone.
Make your journey count, chose wisely.
And live a life extraordinary, anyone can be ordinary.

Ann T. Fenelon
12-14-01

Systems Melt Down

Computer over load-
Brain on fire-
Documents in distress-
()&^%$#%&^((&*&&
#%*)*&%#@$%*)()(*&^#$%

Don't panic.
Don't delay.
Call trouble-shooters,
Right away-

"Control Panel"
"Control Panel, did you say."
"See it."
"Got it, yea! yea!, ok."
****
****

If you can read this message; your system is
functioning properly.

A major system malfunction, has been curtailed.
All systems go.

Thank you, GOD!!!!!!!!!
For the trouble-shooter-
ALL SYSTEMS GO!

Ann T. Fenelon
11-18-01

Surrender

Giving in,
Giving up,
To love,
To life,
Happiness,
When you surrender to the universe-
You surrender to the possibility of GOD.

Only through surrender is God made real.
By giving over our "free will",
This if we believe, comes from GOD.
Then and only then,
Are we truly Free!

Giving in, to the love of God,
Giving up, and letting go, to God's Will.
To except, the love of God, into our lives,
And to expect life's unpredictability,
Is the only way to achieve true happiness.

And happiness is the true gold in life.
Enjoying the ride, and making the journey.
Take the time, and surrender to life.
You won't have any regrets.
When this life ends, we will truly begin to live.

Surrender.

A.T.F.
11-21-01

Tell Me Way

Did I not give you all my love?
Did I not tell you all my secrets?
Did I not fulfill all your needs?

Then tell me way we had to end.
I made no demands no you time.
What you gave I gladly accepted.

No questions did I ask.
I made room for you.
In my heart, my life, and my home,

But you still needed more and I gave more.
Cut back on time with my friends.
Spent lees time with my family,

And give that time to you.
Only to have you tell me.
"I fill that I'm being neglected."

Will I've given all I can.
And gone as far as I can,
This trip is over.

Collect your bag at the door.
Don't call me I'll call you.
Six month's later I do.

Just to see how you're doing.
Is life any better for you.
Have you found someone new.

"No, spending time with myself."
Then you tell me how you needed to find your center.
And work on you heart.

And then you ask me.
"When my soul search is over can we try again."
I think about the good times and the bad.

I know I want to try again.
And say so.
"Search long and hard then come home to me."

I don't know if we will be able to move past the past.
I know that I want to try.
When the love was right between us, we worked.

And for the life of me no one can tell me way.
I need to know that my love as not given in vain.
When you give all of your heart and it doesn't work,

You need to know why.
Love is a question in action.
And it should have an answer.

Ann T. Fenelon
12-25-01

The Call

When life opens door
I tend to walk through.
When you called after
Ten years,
I said yes to dinner.

As beautiful as the first day,
I saw you.
Sun light in your hair,
Eye like dark velvet,
And skin as soft as
Fine linen,
My heart stopped cold,
And I could not breathe.

Your hand so warm
In mine,
As we kissed hello,
I was 27, again.
Falling in love,
With you was just that easy.

Minutes into conversation,
And the years dissolve.
I know I still love you.
Will love you always,
And time will never stop
This truth,
You are in my soul.

Married with children,
And happy-
I ask to see pictures.
I'm happy for you.
Love has that way.
Turns heartbreak,
Into joy,

It makes all things,
Right.
I tell you about my new
Love.
Hold your hand a little
To long.

After dinner I walk,
You to your hotel.
We promise to keep in touch.
Maybe, this time we can.
Love makes all things,
Right.

Ann T. Fenelon
1-16-02

Sunshine

Crystal skies,
Split open.
Brilliant burst of light.
Havens glory on display.

Reason enough
To smile.
A break from winters chill.
Melts the snow away.

A canopy of golden light;
The crowning touch;
Of God's creation.
A woman that knows her place.

Commanding,
In her regal state.
All subjects,
Basking in her grace.

A blessing on the
Human race.
The touch of her warm embrace.
Her genteel smile upon our face.

Ann T. Fenelon
1-26-02

The Magic Of You

Magical thing happen when I'm lying next to you.
Time cease and the troubles of the world seem to dissipate.
Music plays in the air, flowers bloom in the room, and
Rainbows flash in my mind.

I sing around the house and dance while cleaning up.
Never did that before, had I lived or merely existed.
But you've changed my life.
Gave little things meaning, and made me strive for more.

Each day is an adventure.
Each night is a romantic interlude.
Ever time I'm with you is like the first.
Exciting and new,

When you hold me in your arms I come alive.
Can this magic last.
Can love last the test of time on all four burners?
Or will it consume itself and die.

This is always my problem in love.
I tend to over analyze love.
Not this time, so for now you can be Houdini.
And I can assist you; I'll climb up into your box.

And you can separate my logical mind;
From my desirous body and help me disappear into you.
We can make this magic last.
All we have to do is say the magic words.

I love you.
I love you.
I love you.
Amen.

Ann T. Fenelon
12-21-01

The Eye Of The Storm

Did it happen all at once?
Or, was it a gradual thing?
Life has away of sneaking up on you.
Wake up and you're forty.
And you don't even remember how you got here.

Caught in the eye of a storm,
Life moves with force.
In the center of your being,
Life holds calm.
While all around you, the world spins out of control.

I still hear that voice inside myself.
It tells me that life holes all the answers.
If we can learn to ask the right questions,
Then we will live up to our potential.
I hear the voice.

I still don't know the right question.
Or, I just don't want to ask it.
I like not knowing the answers.
I like the edge.
I live there as a tribute to my spirit.

That desire in me.
The reason I wake each day.
And try.
To move one-step closer, to myself,
And the only question I need to ask is.

Do I love myself enough to remove doubt?
To take away all fear.
Fear stifles my growth.
I abandons my soul.
I leave the eye of the storm and spin out of control.

Ann T. Fenelon
12-31-01

The Sweet Lowdown

What's the word on the street.
What's the sweet lowdown.
The funky blues that walks down the street,
And sings a song so low and so-so-sweet,
To rock my soul and make me dance.

Baby it's you.
Always has been, always will be.
My sweet-sweet lowdown honeydew,
The music in my head is all about you.
You are the music of my heart and soul.

The reason why I sing in the shower,
In the morning, and dance my way to work.
The reason I smile all day.
And pray for the weekend to come.
So I can see you face, for an uninterrupted rendezvous.

And the music is always blue.
Slow-low-sweet-melodic melody,
The rhyme of our love song,
That we alone can play.
It's all about the music, the song of you and me.

Ann T. Fenelon
12 13 01

The Best Of Times

Does a child with a gun become an adult?
When another child dies by the gun he holds.
In the best of times, we suffer the pain of innocence.

In the best of times, we suffer the madness of the world.
When children bring guns to schools to kill each other,
And we in turn sentence them to death.

Instead of finding the cause of the problem,
We seek revenge on the smallest victims, in this nightmare.
And we perpetuate the endless suffering of society.

We need to step back, and help children be children.
Start by taking guns out of their hand.
Which means we must stop the flow of guns in society.

We have to take responsibly for each other.
We must stop putting blame, on TV, and Movies.
We must stop putting the role of adult on the shoulders,

Of our children, who already have in hard in life.
We rush our children into adulthood.
And we blame them when they fall short.

What we teach they learn.
If we do not teach compassion,
Our children will never learn compassion.

And we do teach by example.
If we kill our children today, what will become of us.
Will we have a future, or will that future be worthwhile living.

Is this the best of times or the worst.
Is the future bright or cast in a pall.
And what will become of our children, our future hope.

Ann T. Fenelon
12-05-01

U.S. Open

Day 4 and the rain come down.
Holding up play,
Brings down my high.
I'm in need of a
V. Williams fix.

"Advantage Williams"
Is my Open fix.
S. Williams or V.,
Just gets me high.
U.S.A. is my cry.

But, the rain man she come on down.
Her carry me way-way low.
Me heart is heavy and beat real slow.
I need hear "Advantage Williams",
To take me way up high.

If I see Pete or André, I may get by.
But, Williams vs. Williams is a natural high.
So, rain-rain go a way.
Must see Open TENNIS today.
V. Williams, S. Williams, All The Way!!!

Ann T. Fenelon
8-29-02

Water Of Life

We are born from water.
We exist in a world dependent on its life force.
We live and die in its embrace.

It calls us into being.
Like the rush of the wind, we are propelled;
Into this world through the birth cannel,
By water we are born.

Just as man began, by washing ashore from the sea,
So many years ago, by water were we born.

We drown in the sadness of our own tears.
We agonize in a thirst that it alone can quench.

We are sustained by the harvest it produces.
And divested by its ravage force as rain,
Snow, hail, and flood, we are destroyed.

It refreshes us with our morning shower;
Relaxes us in our evening bath,
Invigorates us as we walk along the beach,
In a gentle rain, we are born-again.

We flow in its stream of life.
In a church fount we are blessed by water.
At our funeral mass we are blessed by water.
As we lay in our grave,
By heaven's rains we are blessed by water.

At the end of life we are called to that shore;
Where all life begins,
We wade, out to sea, to wash ashore.
On some long forgotten beach,
Where a new journey awaits us,
And by water we are born.

Ann T. Fenelon
12-09-01

Walking On Water

I'm no miracle worker.
No wonders do I perform.
I'm only human.
Please see me as human.
With many faults,
The biggest fault I have is loving you to much.

In your eyes I have become superhuman.
A 'god' who can do no wrong-
I'm no GOD!
I can disappoint you, and I have.
For this I'm truly sorry.
Please forgive me.

Love me as I love you faults and all.
When I look at you I see only you.
I never go beyond the person you are.
I never ask you for more then you can give.
But you expect me to work miracles.
To walk on water-

And turn that water into wine.
It's not me, never has been never will be.
Day in and day out I do my very best to make you happy.
But my best is not good enough.
So you decide.
Love me as I'm or leave me.

I would take you!
I love you unconditionally.
Why can't you love me the same?
Give me the same respect.
I love you, and want you in my life.
So the question is do you really love me.

Do I have to walk on water for your love?
Can't we just be two fools in love.
You loving me, just as I' am.
And I will try to be a better person, for you each day.
Not 'god-like', just a better person.
I am just a simple person, who loves you, with all my heart.

Ann T. Fenelon
12-01-01

Weightless

I walk on the edge of life weightless.
I refuse to participate.
I never take a stand on one side or the other.

I'm indifferent; there is no black-white-or gray.
Its not that I don't care, I care too much.
To the point of pain, I care.

It leaves me numb inside.
I can't cry if I start I would never stop.
So I stand on the threshold.

I'm unable to enter and to stubborn to turn away.
I'm frozen, weightless, at lost in the reality of life.
No prayer of hope can answer this enigma.

But I do pray.
If only for hope in God, in faith, in life,
I pray.

And I wait.
To feel something real,
A pin prick, to pop my soul and make me live.

To be grounded in reality.
To be sown into the tapestry of life.
I pray.

Each day I pray.
Every night I pray.
And I wait, for the answer.

That will save me.
From this state of weightlessness,
That makes me numb to life.

For help to cross that threshold,
That takes me from witness.
To participant of life, a human being,

Who lives life to the fullest!
Who walks on the edge but lives in the moment;
And finds hope in the simple reality of life.

Ann T. Fenelon
12-07-01

Night Fall

When night is falling
And your love calling
My heart sweet darling
Will open to you,

A place you find with
Love divine. My heart
Will incline your sweet
Heart divine,

And morning light
Soft and bright will
Melt with mine,
Each sweet noon
Time;

When night is falling
Will be our love
Rhyme.

Ann T. Fenelon
11/4/2001

Wild Cherry

Cordate drupe
Sweet stone fruit.

Plucked from the tree
At just the right moment
By fingers rubbing dust away.

Teeth tearing tight skin
Exposing rich burgundy flesh.
Wild juice caresses in the mouth,
Tongue licking lips for every drop.

Hungry, teeth feed on the fleshy
Meat, to the center, the pit.
Biting through the black-red hull
To reach the heart's bitter-sweet droplets.

One moment of ecstasy.

Ann T. Fenelon
11-28-01

Written On The Heart

Champollion made use
Of the Rosetta Stone,
To decipher ancient walls.
I hold no such key,
To your heart.

If only I could
Discern these messages.
The hieroglyphs of your heart.
Which hides all pain.
But, I stumble blindly through

Your heart.
Unable to create
A safe-home
For you.
You refuse,

To share your pain.
I sense with my own
Emotions the absence
Of you soul.
The reasons,

Why you cry at night,
And conceal you tears
From me.
Still, I stand ready.
Let me be your safe harbor.

Reveal your heart to me.
Let me keep your secrets.
Heal your pain,
And help you,
Restore your soul.

Ann T. Fenelon
1-09-02

Windstorm

The wind ripped
Through the canyon.
Spilling air in great
Huffs.
Calling up the dust.
It whirred,
In cyclonic proportion.

We huddled near
The face of the mountain.
Shielding our eyes.
I could feel the
Pounding of your heart.

Pulling you closer
Kissing your dusty cheek.
You relaxed the beat
Of your heart.
In the safety of my arms.

Later,
In the cabin, we shower.
Washing the dust from
Our hair and bodies.
I hold you close,
Feel the anxious thump,
Of your heart.

I smile and kiss your cheek.
Knowing,
Not fear but desire
Rules your heart.
We start a whirlwind
Of our own.

Ann T. Fenelon
1-28-02

Winter

Ice crystals form on my windowsill.
Announce the official arrival of Winter.
I snuggle down deep under my downy comforter.
Enraptured in my flannel gown,
Present from my sister,
I sleep the whole night, safe and sound.

The winds whip and whistle is my lullaby.
In the morning a simple touch of the window.
Determines my days dress,
I ware my black turtleneck shirt.
Black Jeans, black leather jacket and black boots,
I love Winter it brings out the spy in me.

I make my way to the train;
I hole myself close for extra warmth.
Listen to others complain of the cold.
And they wish for the return of Summer.
Not me, the crisp cool fresh smell,
Of Winter air, invigorates ever pore of my body.

Hot spicy Lentil soup for lunch, at Café Creole,
Fill my body with Winter's warmth.
Warm bread and hot lemon tea round off the meal.
I retrieve my shades from my jacket pocket.
Zip up my leather and exit out to Winter.
I smile as I make my way down the street.

Ann T. Fenelon
12-29-01

You Alone

Your touch
The warmth of your caress,
Is all I live for.
Hold me in your arms.
Love me.

Tell me our love,
Will last.
Lie to me if you must.
If only for tonight.
Make me believe in forever.

With your hands,
Your kisses,
Your mouth,
Make me believe in you.
Paint me a picture,

Of paradise.
We sit on the bank,
Of a stream.
Watching the sunlight dance,
On the ripples of the water.

And make love
To the songs of Blue Jays
Flying by.
Sip warm wine from the bottle.
Eat fresh figs from a tree.

Dream the day away,
In paradise.
You are my paradise.
My safe corner.
Only you and you alone.

Ann T. Fenelon
1-14-02

Tightrope Walker

Loving you is like walking on fire.
One day you're hot as hell.
The next you're cold as ice.
Sometimes I don't know
If I'm coming or going.

I feel that I'm up
On the high wire all alone.
That I'm the only one
Invested in this
Relationship.

How can this be?
When I go to sleep
With you next to me
Each night.
We love each other.

But, in the morning
You're unrecognizable.
The face is the same
Face I adore.
Your heart is just not

With me.
I walk around on eggshells.
I'm afraid to say or do
Something that will
Pull you even farther

Away from me.
I'm not ready to walk
Away from this love.
I need you to open up.
Let me in your heart.

Meet me half way.
I can dance on the wire.
If I know, you're waiting;
For me when I'm back
On the ground.

Ann T. Fenelon
2-07-02

Time

God's keeper-
Clock reader-
Widow maker-
The hand has moved.

Worlds fall at you feet.
Oceans turn to desert.
Desert turns to sea.
The hand moves once more.

All forgiven,
And forgotten,
Once the hand has written,
It moves on.

Day in and out,
Centuries old and new,
Call you master.
And yet you move on.

For no man holds,
You interest long.
In the blink of an eye,
You are gone.

Ann T. Fenelon
1-07-02

To The Dream

Dear Martin,
Has the dream died?
When two young boys
Kill another young boy,
Because he is Black,
And lives in Colorado,
Your dream has died.

In New York,
41, bullets rain down
On an innocent young Black man
Because, four-white-cops,
See a wallet as a gun.
The dream don't live here
No more.

In Jersey,
Cops shot
At a van load of Black men.
Profiled.
Black men in van equals:
Drug dealers with guns.
All four injured; fortunately, no one died--no drugs, no guns.

Your dream has become
A nightmare.
Oh Martin,
The whole world
Mourns for you.
We cry for ourselves.
We all need to dream a New Dream.

Ann T. Fenelon
1-20-21

Translucent Light

RADIANT SPIRIT
GLEEFUL GHOST
MESSANGER OF TIMES-
LONG PAST,

MOURNFUL GHOST-
FEARFUL HOST-
OF ALL THAT WE SEE,
AND ALL THAT WE DO NOT-

SEE.
WHAT NEWS OF VALHALLA,
AND ODIN, DO YOU BRING.
WHAT WHISPERS OF UNKNOWN-

PERIL,
AND CHANCE FOR REDEMPTION.
DO NOT TRIFLE, WITH MY SOUL.
DO NOT LINGER, IN MY ROOM.

SPEAK THE WORDS OF HEAVEN.
OR CARRY ME TO HELL.
OPEN MY HEART, TO GLADNESS.
OR CLOSE MY SOUL, FOR ALL ETERNITY.

A.T.F
11-16-01

Translucent Moon

Pale moon light,
Angels glow in thy sight.
Lovers howl with delight.
To view you're pristine hallow,
In the night.

Songs, written for you.
World turns to see you.
Thieves in the night avoid you.
The tide races to meet you.
Morning light is sometimes

Blessed to greet you.
The coldest night made warm.
A longing heart made calm.
The sun smiles upon your face.
All the stars in heaven hold your place.

From sea to sea, sailors seek your face.
To guide their way back home.
If not for thee.
Romeo would never know his Juliet.
On that balcony.

The world would spin and spin for naught.
Lovers could never park.
To kiss the night away.
The night sky would dim in despair.
Absent, your loving light.

Ann T. Fenelon
02-02-02

Veiled Lady

Fair Moon Queen,
Beguiling songstress,
Moonlight rider.

Midnight lover,
Rap me in your veil.
Bewitch me with your sirens song.

Taunt my soul to madness.
Bring me to your land of dreams.
Where I gladly surrender to your touch,

Reveal thy face;
Make known thy name;
And love me freely.

As I now love you.
Take me in thy arms, and heart.
And hold me tenderly to thy soul.

Sprinkle star dust on my pillow.
Whisper words of love to me.
Open the depths of my soul with thy touch.

Take me on your golden steed to lands of wonder.
Rap me in your veil, and hide me in your love.
Save me with thy love.

Unveil your face, and trust in me.
Speak your name to me.
I will never betray your love.

Let me see your eyes and know;
This midnight dream is real.
What the heart envisions in a dream;

The soul creates in reality.
And if I can see your face in my dreams,
I will someday hold your heart in actuality.

Ann T. Fenelon
12-08-01

Printed in the United States
by Baker & Taylor Publisher Services